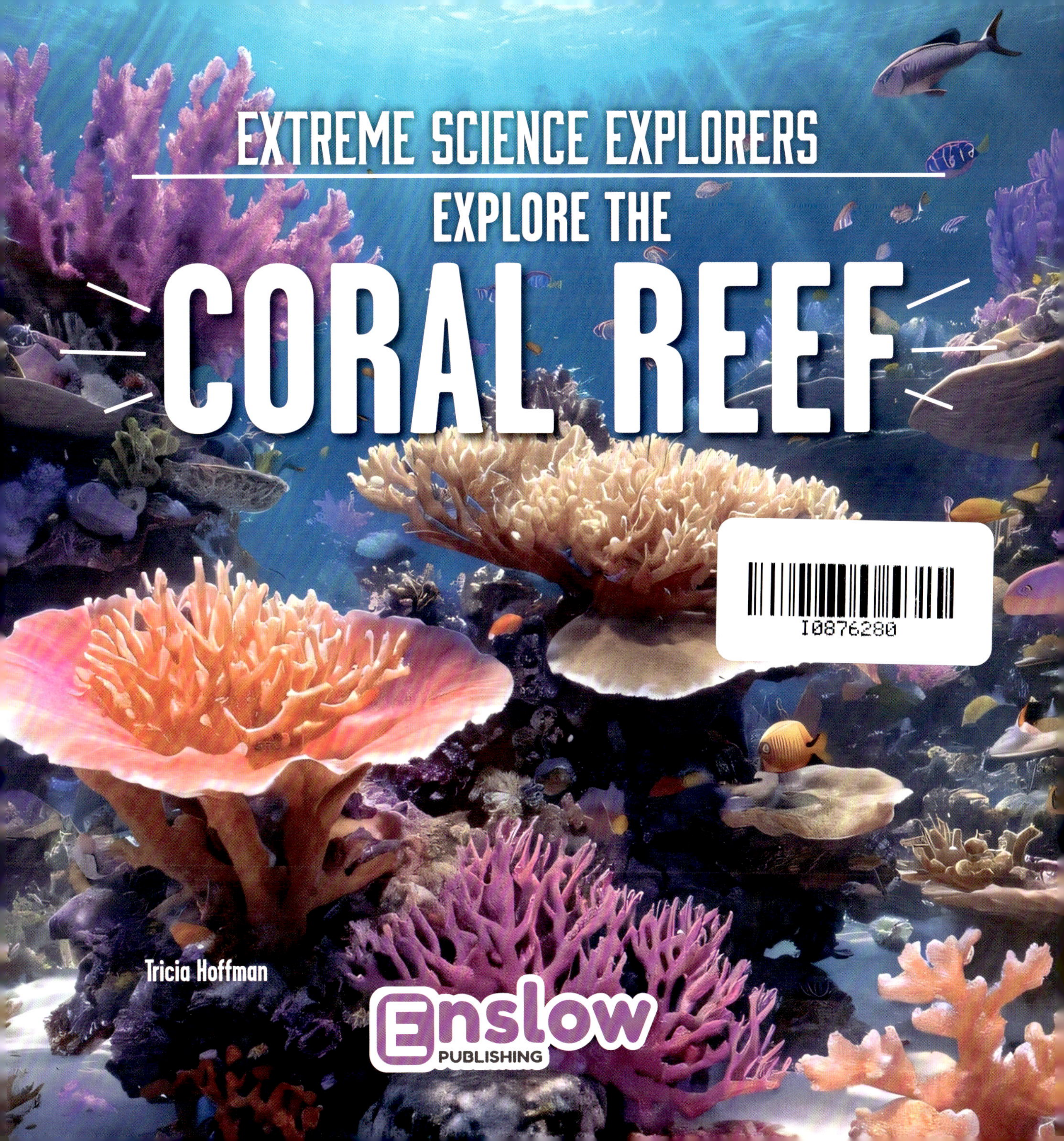

EXTREME SCIENCE EXPLORERS

EXPLORE THE CORAL REEF

Tricia Hoffman

Enslow PUBLISHING

Please visit our website, www.enslow.com. For a free color catalog of all our high-quality books, call toll free 1-800-398-2504 or fax 1-877-980-4454

Published in 2027 by
Enslow Publishing
2544 Clinton Street
Buffalo, NY 14224

Portions of this work were originally authored by Janey Levy and published as *Fantastic Science Journeys: A Trip Through a Coral Reef*. All new material in this edition is authored by Tricia Hoffman.

Cataloging-in-Publication Data
Names: Hoffman, Tricia.
Title: Explore the coral reef / Tricia Hoffman.
Description: Buffalo, NY : Enslow Publishing, 2027. | Series: Extreme science explorers | Includes glossary and index.
Identifiers: ISBN 9781978548992 (pbk.) | ISBN 9781978549005 (library bound) | ISBN 9781978549012 (ebook)
Subjects: LCSH: Coral reefs and islands--Juvenile literature. | Coral reef ecology--Juvenile literature.
Classification: LCC GB461.H644 2027 | DDC 577.789--dc23

Printed in China

Photos Credits: Cover, p. 1 Sarvalokacharine/Shutterstock.com; p. 3 sergey kolesnikov/Shutterstock.com; p. 4 stockphoto-graf/Shutterstock.com; p. 6 Solarisys/Shutterstock.com; p. 7 from-ishigaki/Shutterstock.com; p. 8 Ethan Daniels/Shutterstock.com; p. 10 tank200bar/Shutterstock.com; p. 11 Levent Konuk/Shutterstock.com; p. 12 Isra.hong/Shutterstock.com; p. 12 dvlcom - www.dvlcom.co.uk/Shutterstock.com; p. 13 Ethan Daniels/Shutterstock.com; p. 14 WindVector/Shutterstock.com; p. 14 John A. Anderson/Shutterstock.com; p. 16 Mathias Berlin/Shutterstock.com; p. 18 Crystal Eye Media/Shutterstock.com; p. 18 Jonas Gruhlke/Shutterstock.com; p. 20 Spotmatik Ltd/Shutterstock.com; p. 22 Richard Whitcombe/Shutterstock.com; p. 23 Rich Carey/Shutterstock.com; p. 23 Sergey Skleznev/Shutterstock.com; p. 23 Azrael3141/Shutterstock.com; p. 23 RLS Photo/Shutterstock.com; p. 23 Rich Carey/Shutterstock.com; p. 23 AmyWilliamsPhotography/Shutterstock.com; p. 24 EB Adventure Photography/Shutterstock.com; p. 27 Angela N Perryman/Shutterstock.com; p. 28 MilanMarkovic78/Shutterstock.com; p. 29 Nicole Helgason/Shutterstock.com; p. 31 Hangoverr/Shutterstock.com

CPSIA compliance information: Batch #QSENS27: For further information, contact Enslow Publishing, New York, New York, at 1-800-398-2504.

TABLE OF CONTENTS

GET READY TO EXPLORE

Coral reefs are home to thousands of species, including fish, sea turtles, and more. They look like colorful rock gardens in the ocean. They're always growing and changing.

Coral reefs are formed of small sea animals. Corals are tiny animals with soft bodies. They form a hard, cup-shaped outer **skeleton** and stick to the ocean floor, where they live all their life. After they die and their body breaks down, their skeleton remains. Over a long time, these skeletons build up and form reefs.

Exploring a coral reef is a unique and fun experience. Are you ready? Let's go!

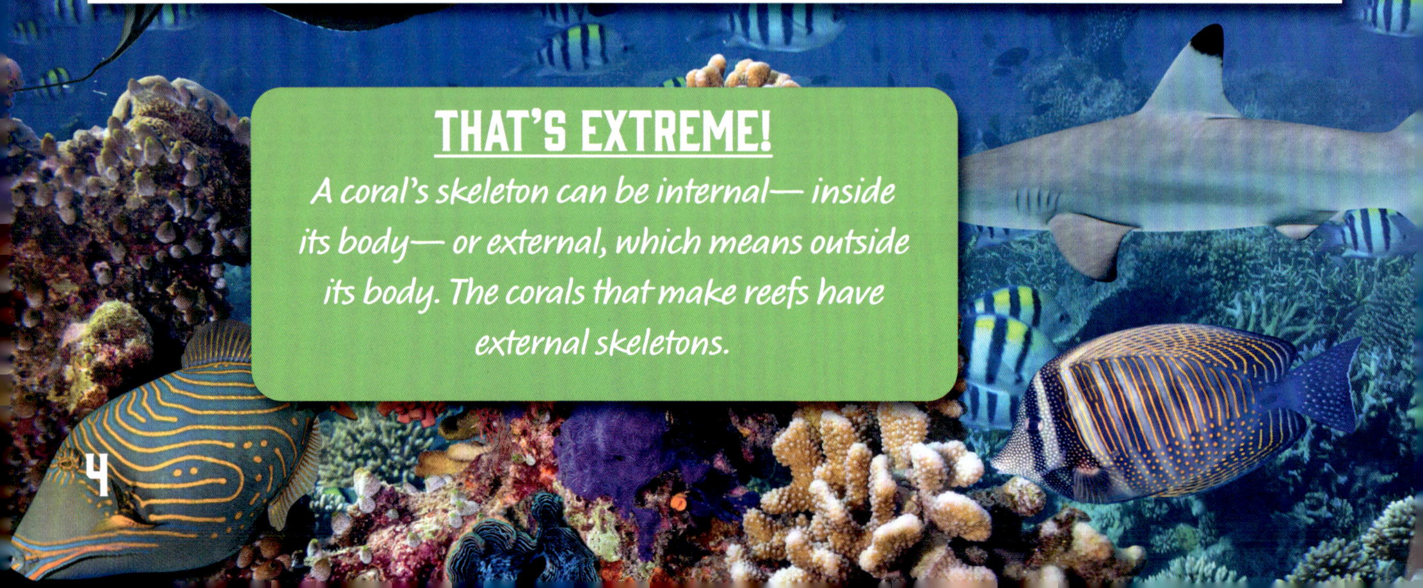

THAT'S EXTREME!

A coral's skeleton can be internal— inside its body— or external, which means outside its body. The corals that make reefs have external skeletons.

Coral reefs are often called the "rainforests of the sea." That's because so much ocean life depends on them.

Coral reefs make up less than 1 percent of the entire ocean floor.

SEARCHING FOR CORAL REEFS

The best place to find coral reefs is along the **equator**. Reefs commonly form near the equator along ocean shores.

Look for shallow water less than 300 feet (90 m) deep. Search for clear water too. Corals need sunlight to live and grow. This water won't have too many nutrients in it. Lots of nutrients make water cloudy, so sunlight can't shine through and coral can't grow.

THAT'S EXTREME!

If corals build up in water that's too shallow, they can dry out and die. They're also in danger of being harmed during storms.

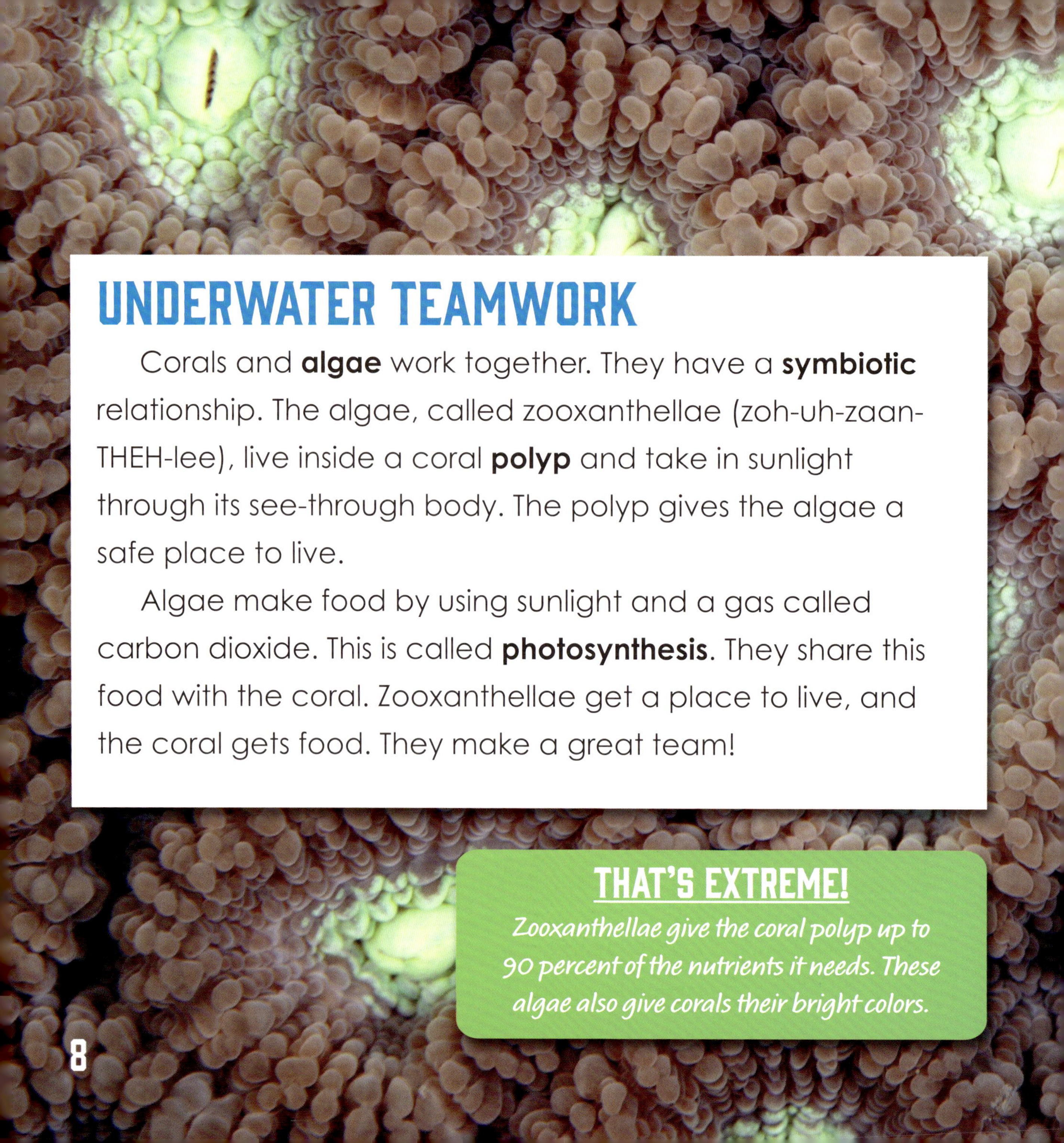

UNDERWATER TEAMWORK

Corals and **algae** work together. They have a **symbiotic** relationship. The algae, called zooxanthellae (zoh-uh-zaan-THEH-lee), live inside a coral **polyp** and take in sunlight through its see-through body. The polyp gives the algae a safe place to live.

Algae make food by using sunlight and a gas called carbon dioxide. This is called **photosynthesis**. They share this food with the coral. Zooxanthellae get a place to live, and the coral gets food. They make a great team!

THAT'S EXTREME!

Zooxanthellae give the coral polyp up to 90 percent of the nutrients it needs. These algae also give corals their bright colors.

There are 6,000 different species of coral in the world.

Some corals have tentacles that can feel the smallest vibrations in water. This lets them catch prey before it gets away.

POISONOUS TENTACLES

Corals have pointy, poisonous **tentacles**. They can be used to grab some tasty treats that might be floating by. Most corals get their food from algae's photosynthesis, but they can also get dinner for themselves. They usually strike for dinner at night.

A coral's tentacles have special stinging cells called nematocysts (nih-MAA-toh-sihsts). They sting like a jellyfish! Corals' most common meal is zooplankton, which are the tiniest animals on Earth. Sometimes corals can snag small fish. The poison in their tentacles can be deadly!

THAT'S EXTREME!

Corals belong to the same animal group as sea anemones (uh-NEH-muh-neez) and jellyfish. Sea anemones are ocean animals that look like flowers.

COLORFUL CORAL

Corals come in all sorts of colors, including shades of blue, purple, green, red, and more. Their coloring comes from the algae living in the coral.

THAT'S EXTREME!

The crown-of-thorns starfish likes to eat living coral so much that it has destroyed some of the Great Barrier Reef. Fish, worms, and snails also munch on polyps.

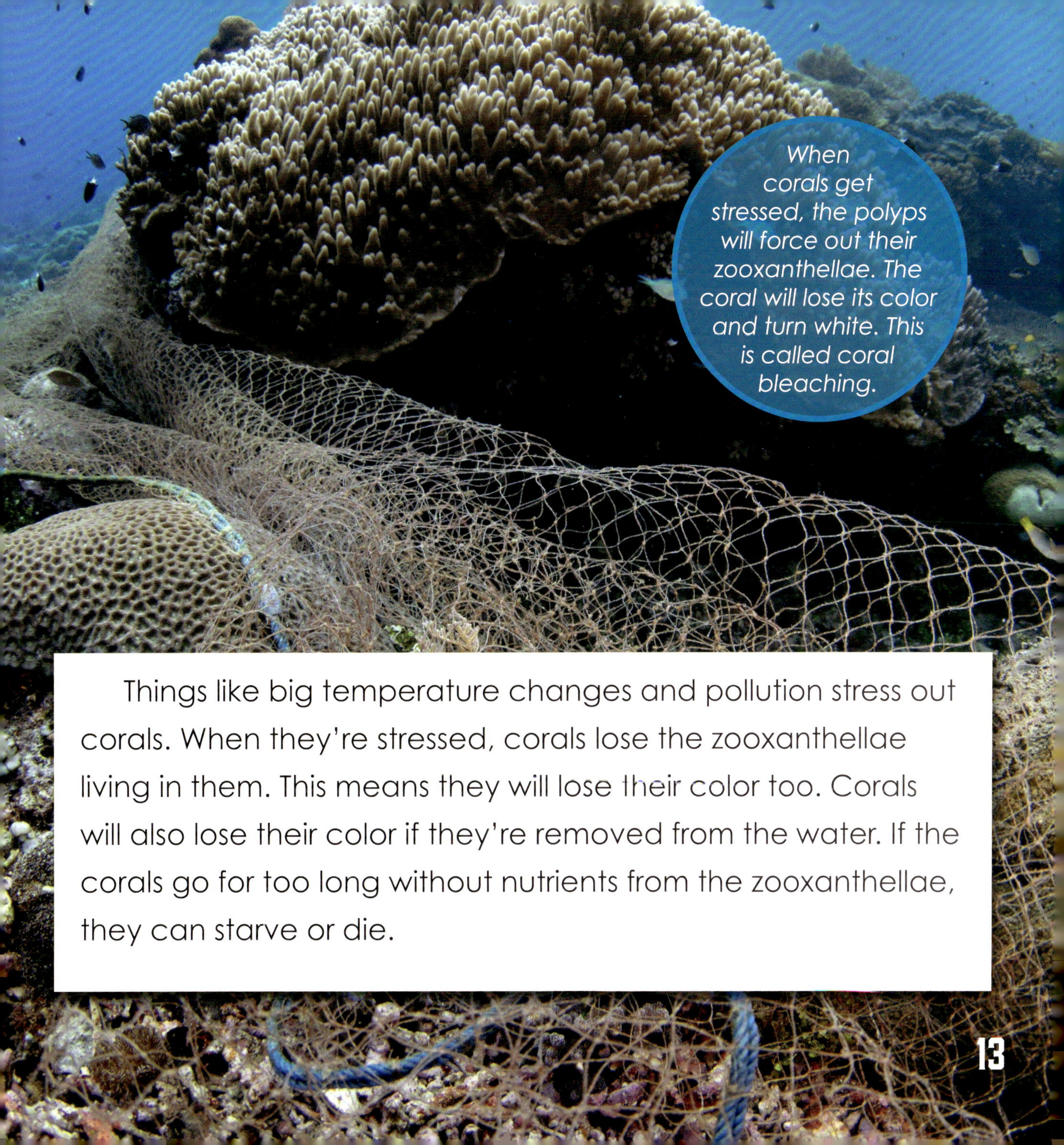

When corals get stressed, the polyps will force out their zooxanthellae. The coral will lose its color and turn white. This is called coral bleaching.

Things like big temperature changes and pollution stress out corals. When they're stressed, corals lose the zooxanthellae living in them. This means they will lose their color too. Corals will also lose their color if they're removed from the water. If the corals go for too long without nutrients from the zooxanthellae, they can starve or die.

HARD CORALS AND SOFT CORALS

Just like their colors, corals also come in all different shapes and sizes. The movement of the water makes the different coral shapes. For example, strong waves make thick or flat coral shapes.

Only a certain kind of coral can form a reef. Reefs are formed from hard shallow-water coral. Common kinds of hard coral include brain, mushroom, pillar, staghorn, and plate (or table) coral.

Soft corals sometimes look like plants or leaves. Soft corals don't form reefs but can be found among them.

THAT'S EXTREME!

The area north of Australia is often called the Coral Triangle. More than 600 kinds of coral grow there.

Brain coral gets its name because it looks like a human brain! It can live up to 900 years.

The Great Barrier Reef is the biggest reef system in the world. It is home to more than 9,000 different species.

KINDS OF CORAL REEFS

There are three main kinds of coral reefs. Fringing reefs are most common and form along the shore. They are located very close to land. Barrier reefs grow farther out from shore. The third type of reef is called an atoll.

The Great Barrier Reef started forming around the end of the last ice age, about 10,000 years ago. It runs 1,400 miles (2,300 km) along the northeastern coast of Australia. It is nearly as big as California!

THAT'S EXTREME!

*About 500 million years ago, supertiny animals called coral polyps lived in some **tropical** waters. They stuck themselves to the ocean floor near the shoreline. That's how the first reefs were born.*

FRINGING REEFS

Reefs form very slowly. They begin when one polyp attaches to the ocean floor. That polyp buds, or divides, into thousands of **clones**. These new polyps attach to one another and form a colony. Little by little, more and more colonies join and build up into a reef.

Fringing reefs are often the first kind of coral reef to form. Over time, and if conditions are just right, they will slowly get bigger and bigger. They can turn into barrier reefs or even atolls.

THAT'S EXTREME!

The Great Barrier Reef isn't just one reef. More than 2,900 smaller reefs make up this amazing reef system!

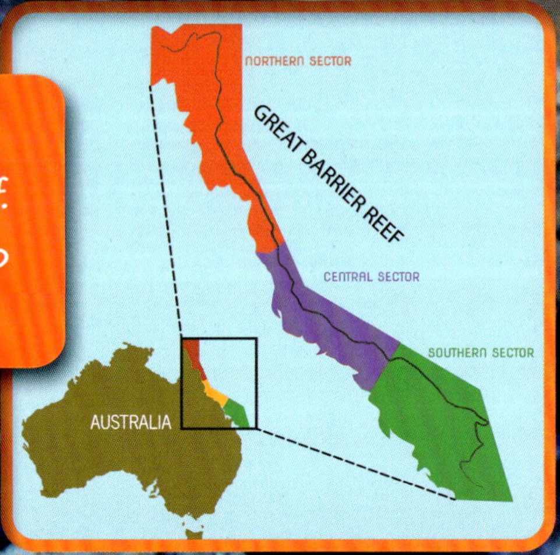

Depending on their size, barrier reefs and atolls can take millions of years to form.

BARRIER REEFS AND ATOLLS

Barrier reefs are formed when a fringing reef gets separated from the shore. Over time as sea levels rise, the land where the fringing reef started growing sinks. A **lagoon** slowly forms next to it and separates the land from the reef to make a barrier reef. It's a long, thin strip that runs along the shoreline. Most of it is underwater.

Tupai is an atoll near Bora Bora. When seen from the air, this atoll is in the shape of a heart.

If sea levels keep rising and falling, the land near the reef may sink so that only the reef can be seen at the surface of the water. This creates an atoll.

THAT'S EXTREME!

The Great Barrier Reef is made up of more than 350 different species, or kinds, of coral.

A CORAL REEF HOME

Reefs are an important source of shelter for animals. Seabirds, sponges, jellyfish, and starfish call coral reefs home. So do shrimp, rays, snails, crabs, lobsters, sea turtles, and sea snakes.

Coral reefs make up less than 1 percent of the ocean floor, but 25 percent of the ocean's animals call those reefs home. More species may not have even been discovered yet!

THAT'S EXTREME!

Coral reefs are some of the most diverse ***ecosystems*** *in the world. So many different animals, all in one place!*

FISH THAT LIVE IN THE REEF

Coral reefs are home to many kinds of fish. Scientists divide these fish into six groups based on how they get their food.

	Group	Fish	Feeding
	**cleaner fish**	cleaner wrass	eat mucus and parasites found on the skin of other fishes
	**herbivores**	surgeon fish	eat algae growing on reef
	**invertebrate predators**	parrot fish	eat coral polyps and other **invertebrates**
	**omnivores**	triggerfish puffers	eat **crustaceans** and reef algae
	**piscivores**	groupers	eat other fish around reef
	**planktivores**	groupers butterfly fish damselfish	feed in large groups feed on plankton found near coral reef

Many people love to explore coral reefs. Coral reefs in the Florida Keys draw millions of visitors each year!

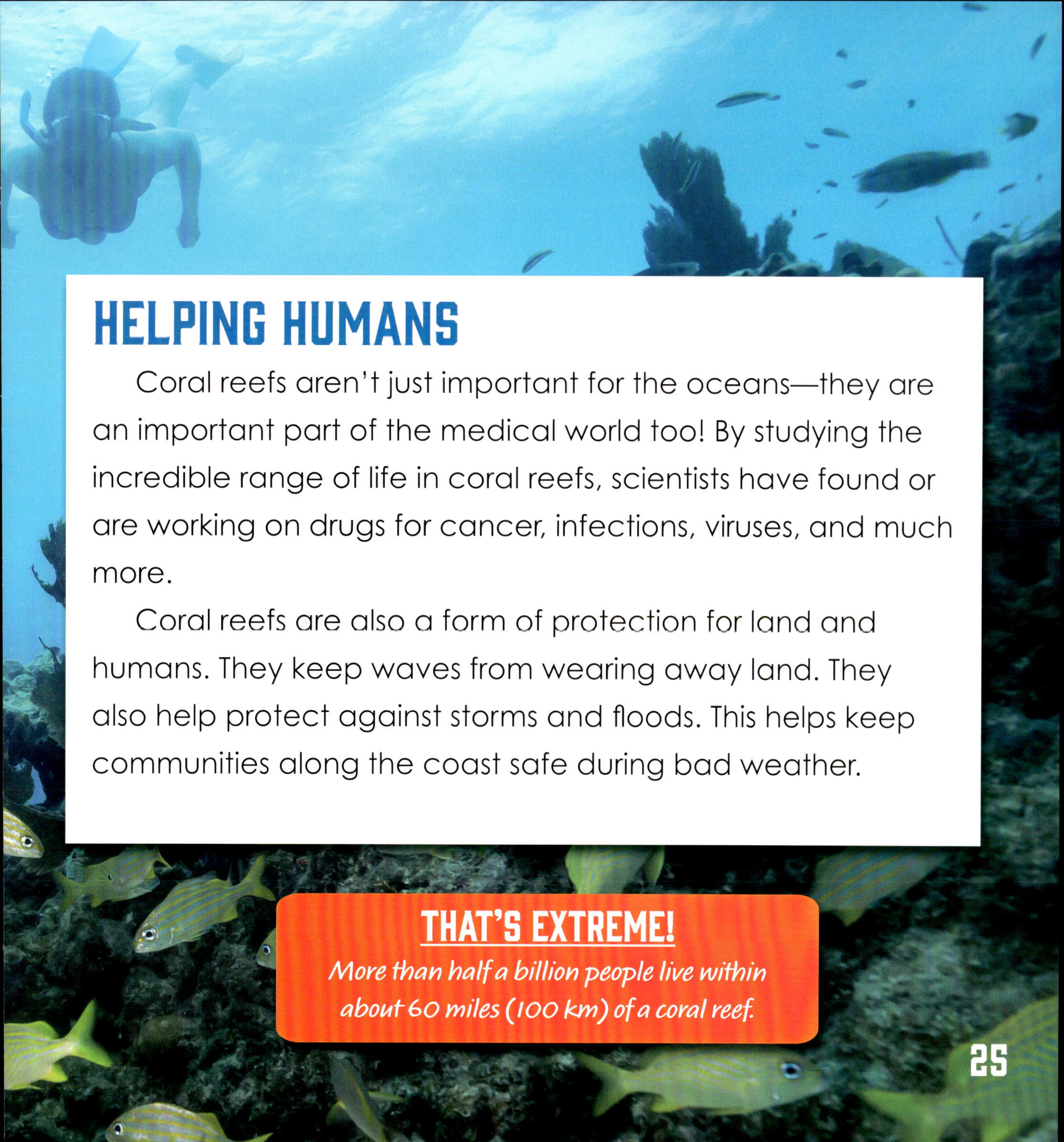

HELPING HUMANS

Coral reefs aren't just important for the oceans—they are an important part of the medical world too! By studying the incredible range of life in coral reefs, scientists have found or are working on drugs for cancer, infections, viruses, and much more.

Coral reefs are also a form of protection for land and humans. They keep waves from wearing away land. They also help protect against storms and floods. This helps keep communities along the coast safe during bad weather.

THAT'S EXTREME!

More than half a billion people live within about 60 miles (100 km) of a coral reef.

GROWING MORE CORAL REEFS

Reefs are an important part of ocean life, and humans have learned how to help reefs grow. At coral farms, polyps are grown and then planted on a healthy reef. The Nature Conservancy has farms off the coast of Florida and in the Virgin Islands that grow coral.

New reefs can also be started on "reef balls." These are hollow balls made of special concrete. They are made to draw coral polyps and other ocean animals. The hollow insides provide shelter for lots of ocean species.

THAT'S EXTREME!

There are 5,000 reef balls already growing coral around the world in more than 59 countries.

Reef balls can float, so they can be easily placed in the ocean by divers or small boats.

Climate change is impacting coral reefs. You can help cut down on climate change by turning off the lights when you're not using them, walking rather than driving whenever possible, and recycling!

SAVE THE CORAL REEFS!

Now that we've explored coral reefs, we know how important they are. Pollution, disease, people, and warming waters are just some of the dangers to coral reefs. People can all work together to help keep the coral reefs healthy. Scientists predict that nearly all reefs will be threatened by 2050 if we don't take action now.

Coral reefs are both beautiful and priceless to humans and animals. They are a valuable part of our oceans and our planet!

THAT'S EXTREME!

Corals sense changes in the weather. Scientists can even use coral reef fossils to learn about the weather millions of years ago.

GLOSSARY

algae: plantlike living things that are mostly found in water

clone: an exact copy of an animal

crustacean: an animal with a hard shell that lives in water

equator: an imaginary line around Earth that is the same distance from the North and South Poles

invertebrate: an animal without a backbone

lagoon: water between the shore and a coral reef

photosynthesis: the process used by plants and algae to make food from sunlight and carbon dioxide

polyp: a single coral animal

skeleton: the strong frame that supports an animal's body

symbiotic: having to do with a relationship in which two parties live together and help one another to live

tentacle: a long, thin body part that sticks out from an animal's head or mouth

tropical: having to do with the warm parts of Earth near the equator

MORE INFORMATION

BOOKS

Burnard, Jane. *A Coral Reef Story*. New York, NY: Kingfisher, 2025.

Pickersgill, Kristie. *Coral Reefs*. London, UK: Usborne, 2025.

Spencer, Erin. *The World of Coral Reefs*. North Adams, MA: Storey Publishing, LLC, 2022.

WEBSITES

Coral Reef
kids.nceas.ucsb.edu/biomes/coralreef.html
Dive in for all kinds of coral reefs, the animals that call them home, and more!

NOAA Coral Reef Conservation Program
coralreef.noaa.gov/
Learn all about coral, coral reefs, and what we can do to protect them.

Publisher's note to educators and parents: Our editors have carefully reviewed these websites to ensure that they are suitable for students. Many websites change frequently, however, and we cannot guarantee that a site's future contents will continue to meet our high standards of quality and educational value. Be advised that students should be closely supervised whenever they access the internet.

INDEX